Table Of Contents

Chapter 2: Content Marketing Techniques for Increased Traffic 1

Chapter 3: SEO Strategies for Local Businesses 1

Chapter 4: Social Media Engagement to Drive Website Visits 1

Chapter 5: Email Marketing Campaigns that Convert 1

Chapter 6: Paid Advertising Tactics for Targeted Traffic 1

Chapter 7: Influencer Partnerships for Enhanced Visibility 1

Chapter 8: Building a Strong Online Community to Boost Traffic ... 1

Chapter 9: Leveraging Video Marketing for Audience Growth 1

Chapter 10: Utilizing Analytics to Optimize Traffic Sources 1

Chapter 11: Creating Shareable Content to Expand Reach 1

Chapter 1: Understanding the Traffic Landscape 1

Chapter 1: Understanding the Traffic Landscape

The Importance of Consistent Traffic

Consistent traffic is a cornerstone of any successful online business, serving as the lifeblood that fuels growth, engagement, and conversion. When a business experiences a steady stream of visitors, it creates opportunities for deeper connections with potential customers. This continuous flow allows for the nurturing of relationships, which is essential in converting casual browsers into loyal patrons. By understanding the significance of consistent traffic, businesses can better position themselves to implement effective strategies that not only attract visitors but also encourage repeat visits.

One of the primary benefits of consistent traffic is the ability to gather valuable data that informs decision-making. With a regular influx of visitors, businesses can analyze patterns in user behavior, demographics, and preferences. This information can guide content marketing efforts, enabling businesses to tailor their offerings to meet the needs and desires of their target audience. By using analytics to optimize traffic sources, companies can refine their marketing strategies, ensuring that they focus on the channels that yield the highest returns.

In addition to data collection, consistent traffic enhances brand visibility and authority. When a website consistently attracts visitors, it signals to search engines that the content is valuable and relevant. This can lead to improved search engine rankings, making it easier for potential customers to discover the business. Moreover, a strong online presence fosters trust and credibility, as users often perceive well-trafficked sites as more reputable. This perception can be a crucial differentiator in competitive markets, where trust plays a significant role in consumer decision-making.

Social media engagement is a powerful tool for driving consistent traffic. By actively participating in conversations and sharing valuable content, businesses can cultivate an online community that encourages ongoing interaction. This engagement not only helps to attract new visitors but also keeps existing customers coming back for more. Utilizing platforms effectively allows businesses to amplify their reach and foster relationships with their audience, ultimately contributing to sustained traffic levels.

Lastly, consistent traffic is vital for maximizing the effectiveness of marketing initiatives. Whether through email marketing campaigns, paid advertising, or influencer partnerships, a steady stream of visitors ensures that these efforts are not in vain. High-quality traffic enhances conversion rates, making each marketing dollar spent more effective. Therefore, by focusing on strategies that build and maintain consistent traffic, businesses can unlock the potential for sustainable growth and long-term success in the digital marketplace.

Types of Traffic: Organic, Direct, Referral, and Paid

Understanding the various types of traffic that can flow to your business is crucial for developing a comprehensive strategy to attract consistent and high-quality visitors. Traffic can be broadly categorized into four primary types: organic, direct, referral, and paid. Each type serves a unique purpose and can significantly impact your overall marketing strategy. Recognizing the differences among these types will allow you to tailor your approach to maximize visitor attraction effectively.

Organic traffic refers to visitors who find your website through search engine results, often due to effective SEO techniques and high-quality content. This type of traffic is vital for long-term success as it is generally seen as the most valuable due to its sustainability and lower acquisition cost. By optimizing your site for relevant keywords, creating informative and engaging content, and building backlinks, you can enhance your visibility on search engine result pages. This approach not only attracts visitors but also establishes your authority in your niche, leading to increased trust and credibility among your audience.

Direct traffic consists of visitors who type your website URL directly into their browser or access it through their bookmarks. This type of traffic indicates that you have a strong brand presence and that users are aware of your business. Building a solid brand through consistent messaging, quality content, and effective engagement strategies can enhance direct traffic. Additionally, implementing strategies such as memorable domain names and offline marketing efforts can encourage users to visit your site directly, fostering a loyal customer base that returns repeatedly.

Referral traffic comes from other websites, blogs, or social media platforms that link to your content. This type of traffic is essential for expanding your reach and tapping into new audiences. By collaborating with influencers, participating in guest blogging, and engaging in social media partnerships, you can generate valuable referral traffic. It is also important to create shareable content that encourages users to link back to your site. This can include infographics, articles, or videos that offer unique insights or entertainment, further boosting your visibility across various platforms.

Paid traffic involves visitors who arrive at your site through paid advertising efforts, such as pay-per-click (PPC) campaigns, social media ads, or display advertising. This type of traffic can provide immediate results and targeted reach, making it a powerful tool for businesses looking to attract high-quality visitors quickly. Developing effective paid advertising strategies requires a clear understanding of your target audience and continuous optimization based on analytics. By investing in paid campaigns, you can not only increase traffic but also drive conversions when combined with well-structured landing pages and compelling calls to action.

Incorporating a mix of these traffic types into your marketing strategy is essential for unlocking an unstoppable flow of visitors to your business. Each type has its strengths and can complement the others when used effectively. By mastering the art of balancing organic, direct, referral, and paid traffic, you can create a robust system that attracts consistent, high-quality visitors, ultimately leading to greater success and growth in your business.

Key Metrics for Measuring Traffic Success

Key metrics play a crucial role in understanding the success of your traffic generation efforts. By measuring specific indicators, businesses can gain valuable insights into what strategies are working and where improvements are needed. The primary metrics to consider include traffic volume, source of traffic, bounce rate, conversion rate, and engagement metrics. Each of these metrics provides a unique perspective on how effectively your efforts are translating into actual visits and interactions with your content.

Traffic volume refers to the total number of visitors to your website over a specified period. This metric can help assess the overall effectiveness of your marketing campaigns. A rising traffic volume indicates that your strategies, whether they involve SEO, content marketing, or social media engagement, are successfully drawing visitors to your site. However, it is essential to look beyond just numbers; understanding the sources of this traffic is equally important. Analyzing the channels through which visitors arrive—whether organic search, social media, or paid advertising—can help identify which tactics are the most effective for your specific audience.

Bounce rate is another critical metric that measures the percentage of visitors who navigate away from the site after viewing only one page. A high bounce rate may suggest that visitors are not finding what they expected or that the content is not engaging enough. Reducing bounce rates often involves optimizing landing pages, enhancing content quality, and ensuring that the website is user-friendly. This metric can highlight areas for improvement and guide adjustments to your content and design strategies to keep visitors on your site longer, ultimately increasing the chances of conversion.

Conversion rate is perhaps the most telling metric regarding traffic success, as it measures the percentage of visitors who take a desired action, such as signing up for a newsletter, making a purchase, or downloading a resource. By analyzing conversion rates alongside traffic data, businesses can determine how well their content and offers resonate with their audience. A low conversion rate despite high traffic could indicate that while you are attracting visitors, the content or offer may not align with their needs or expectations. This insight allows for targeted adjustments to improve the effectiveness of your calls to action and overall marketing strategies.

Engagement metrics, such as average session duration and pages per session, provide deeper insight into how visitors interact with your content. High engagement levels often indicate that the content is not only attracting visitors but also retaining their interest. These metrics can help identify which types of content are most appealing to your audience, guiding future content creation efforts. By focusing on both quantitative and qualitative metrics, businesses can develop a comprehensive understanding of their traffic sources, leading to more informed decisions and strategies that foster an unstoppable flow of high-quality visitors.

Chapter 2: Content Marketing Techniques for Increased Traffic

Creating High-Quality Content

Creating high-quality content is foundational to unlocking an unstoppable flow of traffic into your business. High-quality content not only attracts visitors but also engages them, encouraging shares and return visits. The first step in creating such content is understanding your audience. Conduct thorough research to identify their interests, pain points, and preferences. This helps in crafting content that resonates deeply with them, making it more likely to be shared across platforms, thus amplifying its reach.

Incorporating effective content marketing techniques is essential for increasing traffic. Start by developing a content calendar that outlines topics, formats, and publication dates. This ensures consistency and allows for strategic planning around seasonal trends or events relevant to your audience. Diversifying content types—such as blog posts, infographics, videos, and podcasts—can cater to different audience preferences, broadening your reach. Additionally, optimizing each piece of content for SEO is crucial; using relevant keywords, meta descriptions, and engaging headers can significantly enhance visibility in search engine results.

Local businesses can particularly benefit from targeted SEO strategies. Focusing on local keywords and creating content that addresses community-specific issues can attract nearby customers. Additionally, leveraging Google My Business and local directories helps improve your online presence. Regularly updating your content with local insights and events not only keeps it relevant but also positions your business as a trusted local authority, driving more traffic from local searches.

Social media engagement plays a vital role in driving website visits. Creating shareable content is essential; this means crafting posts that are visually appealing and thought-provoking. Encourage your audience to engage by asking questions, running polls, and sharing user-generated content. Collaborating with influencers can also amplify your reach. Partnering with individuals who have a strong presence in your niche can introduce your brand to their audience, bringing in fresh traffic. Influencer partnerships can be a powerful tool for enhancing visibility and credibility.

Finally, utilizing analytics to optimize traffic sources is key to maintaining a consistent flow of visitors. Regularly monitoring metrics such as page views, bounce rates, and time spent on pages can provide insights into what content resonates most with your audience. Use this data to refine your content strategy, focusing on the types and topics that yield the best results. By continuously analyzing and adjusting your approach, you can ensure that your content remains relevant and engaging, ultimately driving sustained traffic to your business.

Content Distribution Strategies

Content Distribution Strategies play a pivotal role in ensuring that your carefully crafted content reaches the intended audience effectively. In an age where information overload is the norm, merely creating high-quality content is not enough. It is essential to have a comprehensive strategy that focuses on how and where to distribute your content to maximize its visibility and engagement. This involves identifying the right channels, understanding audience preferences, and leveraging various platforms to ensure that your message resonates with potential visitors.

Social media platforms are among the most powerful tools for content distribution. With billions of users worldwide, these platforms provide an unparalleled opportunity to share your content with a vast audience. Tailoring your approach to each platform is crucial; what works on Facebook may not be effective on Instagram or LinkedIn. Utilizing features such as stories, reels, and live videos can enhance engagement, while strategic posting times can further boost visibility. Additionally, engaging with your audience through comments and shares can foster a sense of community and encourage organic distribution.

Email marketing remains one of the most effective channels for content distribution, particularly for nurturing leads and maintaining relationships with existing customers. Creating targeted email campaigns that deliver personalized content can significantly increase open and click-through rates. Segmenting your audience based on their interests and behaviors allows for tailored messaging that speaks directly to their needs. Moreover, including strong calls to action and visually appealing designs can enhance user experience and drive traffic back to your website or landing pages.

Collaboration with influencers can amplify your content distribution efforts significantly. By partnering with individuals who have established credibility and a dedicated following in your niche, you can leverage their audience to gain visibility for your brand. Influencers can share your content, provide testimonials, or create original content that features your products or services. This strategy not only enhances visibility but also builds trust with potential visitors who are more likely to engage with a brand recommended by someone they admire.

Lastly, analytics play a crucial role in optimizing your content distribution strategies. By monitoring the performance of your content across various channels, you can gain insights into what works and what does not. Analyzing metrics such as engagement rates, traffic sources, and conversion rates allows you to refine your approach continuously. This data-driven strategy ensures that you are not only reaching your audience but also engaging them effectively, ultimately driving consistent and high-quality traffic to your business.

Blogging and Guest Blogging for Traffic

Blogging serves as a foundational element in driving consistent traffic to your business. By creating high-quality content that resonates with your target audience, you not only establish authority in your niche but also enhance your online visibility. Regularly publishing blog posts on topics relevant to your audience helps attract organic search traffic, as search engines favor fresh, informative content. It is essential to perform keyword research to identify the terms and phrases your potential visitors are searching for, allowing you to tailor your blog posts accordingly. This strategy not only increases your chances of ranking higher in search results but also addresses the specific needs and interests of your audience, making your blog a valuable resource.

Guest blogging is another powerful strategy for expanding your reach and attracting new visitors. By contributing high-quality content to established blogs within your niche, you tap into an existing audience that is already engaged with the subject matter. This approach not only builds backlinks to your own website, which is beneficial for SEO, but also positions you as an expert in your field. When selecting blogs for guest posting, look for sites that have a strong readership and authority in your niche. Crafting compelling articles that provide genuine value to readers will encourage them to visit your site for more insights, thereby increasing your traffic.

To maximize the benefits of both blogging and guest blogging, it is crucial to promote your content effectively. Utilize social media platforms to share your blog posts and guest articles. Engaging with your audience on these platforms can drive traffic back to your website as you build a community around your brand. Additionally, consider using email marketing to notify your subscribers about new blog content or guest posts. This not only keeps your audience informed but also encourages repeat visits, as loyal readers will be more likely to return for fresh content and updates.

Incorporating SEO best practices into your blogging and guest blogging efforts amplifies your traffic potential. Optimize your blog posts with relevant keywords, meta descriptions, and alt text for images. Similarly, when guest blogging, ensure that your author bio includes a link back to your website. Additionally, focus on creating shareable content that resonates with readers. This can include infographics, listicles, or how-to guides that encourage sharing on social media, further expanding your reach and driving traffic back to your site.

Finally, analyzing the performance of your blogging and guest blogging strategies is essential for ongoing improvement. Utilize analytics tools to track traffic sources, user engagement, and the effectiveness of your content. This data will help you understand what resonates with your audience and what doesn't, allowing you to refine your approach over time. By continually optimizing your content strategy based on these insights, you can create an unstoppable flow of traffic to your business, ensuring that you attract high-quality visitors consistently.

Chapter 3: SEO Strategies for Local Businesses

Keyword Research for Local SEO

Keyword research for local SEO is a foundational element that can significantly enhance the visibility of businesses in their specific geographical areas. It involves identifying the terms and phrases that potential customers use when searching for products or services within a local context. By understanding these keywords, businesses can create targeted content that addresses the needs and interests of their local audience, leading to higher engagement and conversions. The goal is to attract quality traffic that is not only relevant but also likely to convert into actual customers.

One effective approach to keyword research is to utilize tools that provide insights into local search behavior. Tools like Google Keyword Planner, Ahrefs, and SEMrush can help identify keyword volume, competition, and related phrases that potential customers may use. Additionally, local-specific keywords often include geographic modifiers, such as city names or neighborhoods. Businesses should consider their unique selling propositions and integrate these local terms into their keyword strategy to ensure they resonate with the audience they aim to attract.

Competitor analysis is another critical component of keyword research for local SEO. By examining the keywords that competitors rank for, businesses can identify gaps and opportunities in their own strategy. This analysis can reveal which local keywords are driving traffic in the industry and help businesses uncover new terms to target. It's essential to focus not only on high-volume keywords but also on long-tail keywords that may have lower competition but are highly relevant to local searches.

Once a comprehensive list of keywords has been compiled, it is crucial to optimize website content around these terms. This involves updating title tags, meta descriptions, headers, and body content to incorporate the selected keywords naturally. Additionally, creating localized content such as blog posts, FAQs, and landing pages can further enhance visibility. By providing valuable and relevant information that aligns with local search intent, businesses can position themselves as authorities in their field, boosting both organic traffic and customer trust.

Finally, monitoring the performance of targeted keywords is vital for ongoing success. Utilizing analytics tools, businesses can track how well their keywords are performing in search results and how they are impacting traffic and conversion rates. This data-driven approach allows businesses to refine their keyword strategy continuously. By staying responsive to changing trends and customer needs, businesses can maintain a competitive edge in their local market and ensure an unstoppable flow of traffic that translates into sustained growth.

On-Page Optimization Techniques

On-page optimization techniques play a crucial role in attracting consistent and high-quality traffic to your website. These strategies focus on enhancing individual web pages to improve their rankings in search engine results and to provide a better user experience. Key components of on-page optimization include optimizing title tags, meta descriptions, header tags, and ensuring that the content is relevant and engaging. By carefully crafting these elements, businesses can significantly increase their visibility and appeal to both search engines and potential visitors.

One of the fundamental aspects of on-page optimization is keyword research. Identifying the right keywords allows businesses to create content that aligns with what their target audience is searching for. Utilizing tools like Google Keyword Planner or SEMrush can help uncover high-volume, low-competition keywords that can be strategically integrated into your content. This not only drives traffic but also ensures that visitors find the information they are seeking, reducing bounce rates and increasing engagement on the site.

Content quality is another vital component of on-page optimization. High-quality, informative, and engaging content keeps visitors on the page longer, which signals to search engines that the page is valuable. Incorporating multimedia elements such as images, infographics, and videos can enhance user experience and make content more shareable. Additionally, regularly updating content to reflect current trends and data can further improve a site's relevance and authority, encouraging both repeat visits and new traffic.

Internal linking is a technique that often goes overlooked in on-page optimization. By strategically linking to other relevant pages within your website, you not only help search engines crawl and index your site more effectively but also guide visitors to explore more of your content. This practice can increase the overall time spent on your site, improve user experience, and enhance the likelihood of conversions, as users discover additional valuable resources that meet their needs.

Lastly, optimizing for mobile devices is essential in today's digital landscape. With a significant portion of web traffic coming from mobile users, ensuring that your website is responsive and loads quickly on all devices is imperative. Google prioritizes mobile-friendly sites in its rankings, making this a critical component of on-page optimization. By focusing on these techniques, businesses can create a robust online presence that attracts consistent and high-quality traffic, ultimately leading to greater success and growth.

Building Local Citations and Backlinks

Building local citations and backlinks is crucial for enhancing your business's online presence and driving consistent traffic. Local citations are references to your business name, address, and phone number (NAP) across various online directories and platforms. These citations help search engines verify your business's legitimacy and location, which is particularly important for local SEO. By ensuring your NAP is consistent across all platforms, you improve your chances of ranking higher in local search results. This not only increases visibility but also fosters trust among potential customers, as they can easily find accurate information about your business.

Backlinks, on the other hand, are links from other websites that point to your site. They are a significant factor in search engine rankings and can enhance your site's authority. Building quality backlinks requires a strategic approach, focusing on obtaining links from reputable local businesses, industry-related websites, and community organizations. Engaging in partnerships with local bloggers or influencers can also yield valuable backlinks while simultaneously boosting your brand's visibility in the local community. This dual approach not only increases traffic but also establishes your business as a key player in your niche.

To effectively build local citations, start by listing your business on popular directories such as Google My Business, Yelp, and Yellow Pages. Ensure that your information is complete and accurate, including categories, services, and images. Additionally, consider niche-specific directories that cater to your industry. Encouraging satisfied customers to leave reviews on these platforms can further enhance your citation profile and attract more visitors. Remember, the more places your business is listed, the higher the likelihood of being discovered by potential customers.

Incorporating backlinks into your content marketing strategy can also drive substantial traffic. Create high-quality, shareable content that addresses local topics or issues relevant to your audience. This could include blog posts, infographics, or videos showcasing your expertise. When other businesses or websites share your content, they provide backlinks to your site, which not only directs traffic but also enhances your credibility in search engines. Collaborating with local organizations for events or sponsorships can result in additional backlinks from their websites, creating a win-win situation for both parties.

Finally, continuously monitor and analyze your citation and backlink profile using tools like Google Analytics and Moz. Track the effectiveness of your local SEO strategies and make adjustments as needed. This ongoing evaluation will help you identify which citations and backlinks are driving the most traffic, allowing you to refine your approach and focus on high-impact opportunities. By consistently building local citations and backlinks, you can create a robust foundation for your online presence, unlocking an unstoppable flow of traffic to your business.

Chapter 4: Social Media Engagement to Drive Website Visits

Choosing the Right Platforms

Choosing the right platforms for your traffic generation efforts is crucial to unlocking a consistent flow of visitors to your business. With numerous channels available, understanding where to focus your energy and resources can significantly impact your success. Each platform offers unique advantages and caters to different audience segments. By assessing your target market, business goals, and content strategy, you can strategically select the platforms that will yield the best results for your specific niche.

In the realm of content marketing, platforms such as blogs, medium articles, and guest posts on reputable sites can enhance your visibility. These platforms not only allow you to share valuable information but also position you as an authority in your field. High-quality content that resonates with your audience is more likely to be shared, increasing your reach. Incorporating SEO strategies into your content will further improve your chances of ranking higher on search engines, making it easier for potential visitors to find you.

Social media engagement is another powerful avenue for driving traffic. Platforms like Facebook, Instagram, Twitter, and LinkedIn offer diverse ways to connect with your audience. Understanding the demographics and behaviors of users on these platforms is essential. For instance, visual content thrives on Instagram while LinkedIn is better suited for B2B interactions. Crafting tailored content for each platform increases engagement and encourages users to visit your website. Regularly analyzing your social media metrics can also inform your strategy, helping you focus on the platforms that drive the most traffic.

Email marketing remains a highly effective method for reaching potential visitors. Building a robust email list allows you to communicate directly with your audience, offering them valuable insights and incentives to visit your site. Platforms such as Mailchimp or Constant Contact simplify the process of managing campaigns. Personalizing your emails and segmenting your audience can lead to higher conversion rates. Combining email marketing with compelling content and special offers can create a powerful synergy that drives consistent traffic to your business.

Finally, leveraging paid advertising and influencer partnerships can further amplify your reach and visibility. Paid advertising on platforms like Google Ads or Facebook Ads allows for targeted campaigns that can attract high-quality visitors. Meanwhile, collaborating with influencers who align with your brand can introduce you to new audiences and build credibility. When choosing platforms for these strategies, consider where your target audience spends their time and which influencers resonate with them. By diversifying your approach across these platforms, you can create a comprehensive traffic generation strategy that ensures a steady influx of visitors to your business.

Crafting Engaging Social Media Content

Crafting engaging social media content is crucial for driving traffic to your business. In an era where attention spans are short, businesses must create content that not only captures interest but also encourages interaction and sharing. The key to achieving this lies in understanding your audience's preferences and tailoring your content accordingly. Engaging social media posts can take various forms, from eye-catching images and videos to thought-provoking questions and polls that invite followers to participate actively. By focusing on what resonates with your target audience, you can cultivate a loyal following that amplifies your reach.

Visual elements play a significant role in social media engagement. Posts that incorporate high-quality images or videos consistently outperform text-only updates. Infographics, behind-the-scenes videos, and user-generated content can enhance your brand's authenticity and foster a sense of community. To maximize engagement, consider employing storytelling techniques that evoke emotions and connect with your audience on a personal level. This approach not only makes your content more relatable but also encourages sharing, which can exponentially increase your visibility across platforms.

In addition to visual appeal, the timing and frequency of your posts are vital for maintaining engagement. Analyzing when your audience is most active can help you determine optimal posting times, ensuring that your content reaches them when they are most likely to engage. However, it's essential to strike a balance; flooding your followers' feeds may lead to disengagement. A consistent posting schedule that offers a mix of promotional content, educational material, and entertaining posts can keep your audience interested without overwhelming them.

Utilizing interactive features available on various social media platforms can further enhance engagement. Polls, quizzes, and live Q&A sessions provide opportunities for real-time interaction, making followers feel valued and heard. These features not only encourage participation but also provide valuable insights into your audience's preferences and behaviors. By fostering a two-way dialogue, you can build a stronger relationship with your community, which can lead to increased loyalty and, ultimately, more traffic to your business.

Finally, monitoring and analyzing the performance of your social media content is essential for ongoing improvement. Utilize analytics tools to track engagement metrics such as likes, shares, comments, and click-through rates. This data can reveal what types of content resonate best with your audience, allowing you to refine your strategy over time. By continuously adapting to your audience's preferences and leveraging insights from your analytics, you can create a cycle of engagement that drives consistent and high-quality traffic to your business.

Analyzing Social Media Performance

Analyzing social media performance is a critical aspect of understanding how well your content resonates with your audience and how effectively it drives traffic to your business. Social media platforms offer a wealth of data that can be leveraged to assess engagement levels, audience demographics, and overall reach. By closely monitoring metrics such as likes, shares, comments, and click-through rates, businesses can gain valuable insights into the types of content that perform best. This analysis not only helps identify successful strategies but also uncovers areas that require improvement, ultimately guiding the development of more effective content marketing techniques.

One key component of analyzing social media performance is understanding the differences across various platforms. Each social media channel has its unique audience and engagement style. For instance, Instagram may be more effective for visually-driven content, while Twitter excels with concise, timely updates. By evaluating the performance of your posts on each platform, you can tailor your content to fit the preferences of your audience, ensuring that you attract consistent and high-quality visitors. This targeted approach can significantly enhance the effectiveness of your social media engagement strategies, driving more traffic to your website.

Additionally, utilizing analytics tools can streamline the process of measuring social media performance. Tools such as Google Analytics, Hootsuite, or Sprout Social provide comprehensive data on user interactions and traffic sources. By analyzing this data, you can pinpoint which social media campaigns are generating the most website visits and conversions. This information is invaluable for refining your social media strategy and maximizing the return on investment for your marketing efforts. An ongoing assessment of these metrics allows for real-time adjustments, enabling businesses to remain agile in a rapidly changing digital landscape.

Another important aspect of analysis is benchmarking your performance against competitors. Understanding how your social media engagement stacks up against industry leaders can provide insight into potential gaps in your strategy. Conducting a competitive analysis helps identify best practices that you can adopt while also revealing opportunities to differentiate your brand. By consistently monitoring industry trends and competitor activities, you can position your business to capitalize on emerging opportunities, further enhancing your visibility and traffic flows.

Finally, the role of audience feedback in analyzing social media performance cannot be overstated. Engaging with your audience through comments, polls, and direct messages not only fosters a sense of community but also provides critical insights into their preferences and pain points. This feedback loop allows businesses to adapt their content and marketing strategies in real-time, ensuring that they remain relevant and appealing to their target audience. By prioritizing audience engagement and continuously analyzing performance metrics, businesses can cultivate an unstoppable flow of traffic that is both consistent and high-quality.

Chapter 5: Email Marketing Campaigns that Convert

Building an Email List

Building an email list is a fundamental strategy for creating an unstoppable flow of traffic to your business. Unlike social media platforms that can change their algorithms overnight, your email list is a direct line to your audience that you control. By cultivating a robust email list, you can ensure consistent engagement with your target market, nurture leads, and ultimately drive more traffic to your website. This process involves attracting subscribers through various lead magnets, engaging regularly with quality content, and optimizing your email campaigns to enhance conversion rates.

To begin building your email list, consider offering valuable incentives that resonate with your audience. Lead magnets such as eBooks, exclusive webinars, or discount codes can entice visitors to provide their email addresses. It's essential to understand what your audience values most and align your offerings accordingly. By leveraging content marketing techniques, you can create compelling landing pages that highlight the benefits of subscribing. These pages should be optimized for SEO to attract organic traffic, ensuring that your lead magnets reach a broader audience.

Once you have established your email list, maintaining engagement is key to its growth and effectiveness. Regular newsletters, updates about new content, and personalized offers can keep your subscribers interested and involved with your brand. Segmenting your list based on interests or behaviors allows for targeted messaging, which can significantly improve engagement rates. Consistency in communication helps build trust, making your subscribers more likely to click through to your website and convert into paying customers.

In addition to nurturing your email list, analyzing the performance of your campaigns is crucial. Utilizing analytics tools can provide insights into open rates, click-through rates, and user interactions. This data allows you to refine your strategies and tailor your content to better suit your audience's preferences. By understanding what resonates most with your subscribers, you can adjust your campaigns to drive more traffic and enhance conversion rates, ultimately unlocking the potential for sustained business growth.

Finally, integrating your email marketing efforts with other traffic strategies can amplify your results. Collaborating with influencers, leveraging social media platforms, and utilizing paid advertising tactics can bring new subscribers to your email list. Creating shareable content that encourages readers to forward emails or recommend your brand can further expand your reach. By combining these approaches, you create a synergistic effect that not only builds your email list but also drives consistent, high-quality traffic to your business.

Crafting Compelling Email Content

Crafting compelling email content is essential for engaging your audience and driving consistent traffic to your business. The foundation of effective email marketing lies in understanding your target audience and tailoring your message to meet their needs. Start by segmenting your email list based on demographics, interests, and behaviors. This allows you to create personalized content that resonates with each group, increasing the chances of engagement. By addressing specific pain points or desires, you can position your offerings as the solution they are seeking.

The subject line of your email is the first impression your audience will have, making it a critical element in email marketing. A well-crafted subject line can significantly influence open rates, so it should be attention-grabbing yet informative. Use action-oriented language and create a sense of urgency or curiosity to entice recipients to click. A/B testing different subject lines can provide valuable insights into what resonates best with your audience, allowing you to refine your approach over time.

Once your email is opened, the content must maintain the reader's interest. Begin with a strong opening that connects to the subject line and highlights the value of your message. Use concise and engaging language throughout the email, incorporating storytelling techniques where appropriate. Visual elements, such as images or infographics, can enhance the reading experience and make your content more digestible. Always ensure that your email is mobile-friendly, as a significant portion of users access their emails on mobile devices.

Including a clear call to action (CTA) is crucial for guiding your audience to the next step. Whether it's visiting your website, signing up for a webinar, or making a purchase, your CTA should be prominent and easy to follow. Use actionable language that encourages immediate response, and consider placing the CTA button in multiple locations within the email for greater visibility.

Additionally, creating a sense of exclusivity or offering incentives can motivate readers to take action.

Finally, analyzing the performance of your email campaigns is necessary to understand what works and what doesn't. Utilize analytics tools to track open rates, click-through rates, and conversion rates. This data will help you identify trends and adjust your strategies accordingly. Continuous testing and optimization of your email content will lead to improved engagement and ultimately contribute to an unstoppable flow of traffic to your business. By focusing on crafting compelling email content, you can create a powerful channel for driving consistent and high-quality visitors to your site.

Analyzing Email Campaign Results

Analyzing the results of your email campaigns is crucial for understanding their effectiveness and optimizing future efforts. Start by evaluating key performance indicators such as open rates, click-through rates, conversion rates, and unsubscribe rates. Open rates indicate how well your subject lines perform and whether your audience is engaged enough to open your emails. Click-through rates show how effectively your content encourages readers to take action, while conversion rates reveal the ultimate success of your campaign in driving sales or leads. Unsubscribe rates can provide insights into potential issues with your content or frequency, helping you adjust your strategies accordingly.

Segmentation plays a significant role in improving email campaign results. By analyzing the performance of different segments of your audience, you can identify which groups are most responsive to your messages. This allows for targeted content that resonates with specific demographics, interests, or behaviors. For instance, if you find that a particular segment has a higher click-through rate, you can delve deeper into what content appealed to them and replicate that success in future campaigns. Tailoring your messages not only enhances engagement but also builds stronger relationships with your audience.

A/B testing is another powerful method to analyze and improve email campaign results. By sending two variations of an email to a small portion of your list, you can determine which version performs better. This can be applied to subject lines, email layouts, calls to action, and content types. Once you identify the winning variation, you can send it to the rest of your list, maximizing the effectiveness of your campaign. Regularly conducting A/B tests helps you stay adaptable and responsive to changing audience preferences, ensuring your email marketing remains relevant and effective.

Utilizing analytics tools can significantly enhance your ability to analyze email campaign results. Many email marketing platforms offer built-in analytics that provide detailed reports on various metrics. These insights can help you understand user behavior, such as the times your audience is most likely to engage with your emails. By analyzing these patterns, you can optimize your sending times and frequency, leading to improved engagement rates. Additionally, integrating your email data with broader analytics tools can provide a comprehensive view of how your email campaigns contribute to overall traffic and sales goals.

Lastly, drawing actionable insights from your analysis is vital for continuous improvement. After reviewing the performance metrics, take the time to document what worked and what didn't. Establish a feedback loop where you regularly review past campaigns to inform future strategies. Incorporating lessons learned into your content marketing, SEO, and social media strategies will create a cohesive approach to attracting consistent and high-quality visitors. This ongoing cycle of analysis and adaptation ensures that your email marketing remains a powerful tool in your overarching strategy for driving traffic to your business.

Chapter 6: Paid Advertising Tactics for Targeted Traffic

Understanding PPC and Display Advertising

PPC, or pay-per-click advertising, is a powerful tool for businesses seeking to drive traffic to their websites quickly and effectively. This model allows advertisers to bid on keywords related to their products or services, ensuring their ads appear prominently in search engine results or on relevant websites. Unlike traditional advertising methods, where costs are incurred regardless of engagement, PPC only charges businesses when a potential customer clicks on their ad. This targeted approach not only maximizes marketing budgets but also allows for precise audience targeting, ensuring that ads reach individuals who are actively searching for what the business offers.

Display advertising complements PPC by utilizing visual ads placed on websites, apps, or social media platforms. These ads are designed to capture attention through graphics, videos, or interactive elements, often appearing on sites that align with the target audience's interests. Display ads can be particularly effective for brand awareness and retargeting campaigns, reminding users of products they have previously viewed. By combining PPC with display advertising, businesses can create a comprehensive online presence that not only drives immediate traffic but also builds long-term brand recognition.

One of the key advantages of both PPC and display advertising is the ability to track and analyze performance metrics in real time. Advertisers can monitor click-through rates, conversion rates, and overall ROI, allowing them to make informed adjustments to their campaigns. This data-driven approach enables businesses to refine their strategies continually, optimizing ad spend and enhancing effectiveness. By leveraging analytics, companies can identify which keywords and ad placements yield the best results, ensuring that their marketing efforts align with their goals of attracting consistent and high-quality visitors.

Moreover, integrating PPC and display advertising with other traffic generation strategies can amplify results. For instance, using compelling content marketing techniques in conjunction with these ads can lead to higher engagement rates. When ads link to high-quality content, such as informative blog posts or engaging videos, visitors are more likely to convert into customers. Similarly, social media engagement can support these advertising efforts by promoting the same campaigns, creating a cohesive message that resonates across multiple platforms and drives traffic to the business's website.

Ultimately, understanding PPC and display advertising is essential for businesses looking to unlock an unstoppable flow of traffic. These strategies not only provide immediate visibility but also facilitate a deeper connection with potential customers through targeted messaging and engaging visuals. By mastering these advertising techniques and integrating them with other marketing efforts, businesses can create a robust online presence that consistently attracts high-quality visitors, driving growth and success in an increasingly competitive digital landscape.

Creating Effective Ad Campaigns

Creating effective ad campaigns is a critical component of attracting consistent and high-quality visitors to your business. The foundation of a successful ad campaign begins with understanding your target audience. Conduct thorough research to identify their demographics, interests, and online behaviors. This knowledge allows you to tailor your messaging and select appropriate platforms for reaching them.

Whether your audience is local or global, knowing who they are will guide your creative process and improve engagement rates.

Once you have a clear understanding of your audience, the next step is to craft compelling ad copy and visuals that resonate with them. Your messaging should highlight the unique value propositions of your products or services. Utilize persuasive language and strong calls to action that encourage potential customers to take the desired steps, whether that's visiting your website, signing up for a newsletter, or making a purchase. Visual elements, such as high-quality images or videos, should complement your message and enhance the overall appeal of the ads.

Incorporating a variety of advertising channels can significantly boost the effectiveness of your campaigns. Social media platforms, search engine marketing, and display ads each offer unique advantages. For instance, social media allows for real-time engagement and community building, while search engine marketing targets users actively seeking specific products or services. Additionally, consider using retargeting strategies to re-engage visitors who have previously interacted with your brand but did not convert, as this can lead to higher conversion rates.

To maximize the impact of your ad campaigns, leveraging analytics is essential. Regularly monitor key performance indicators such as click-through rates, conversion rates, and return on ad spend. This data provides invaluable insights into what is working and what isn't, enabling you to make informed adjustments to your campaigns. Testing different ad formats, messaging, and targeting options can help you refine your approach and improve overall effectiveness.

Finally, don't underestimate the power of collaboration and partnerships in enhancing your ad campaigns. Influencer marketing can provide access to new audiences and lend credibility to your brand. By partnering with influencers who align with your values and resonate with your target audience, you can amplify your reach and drive more traffic to your website. Building a strong online community and encouraging user-generated content can further enhance your visibility, creating a cycle of engagement that attracts even more visitors to your business.

Measuring Ad Performance and ROI

Measuring ad performance and return on investment (ROI) is crucial for businesses seeking to attract and retain high-quality traffic. The effectiveness of advertising campaigns can significantly impact your overall strategy, determining which channels yield the best results and how resources should be allocated. By implementing robust measurement techniques, you can gain insights into user behavior, engagement levels, and conversion rates, allowing for data-driven decisions that enhance your marketing efforts.

To effectively measure ad performance, it is essential to define clear objectives and key performance indicators (KPIs) at the outset. These metrics may include click-through rates (CTR), conversion rates, cost per acquisition (CPA), and return on ad spend (ROAS). Establishing these benchmarks allows you to assess how well your ads resonate with your target audience and whether they drive the desired actions. By continuously tracking these KPIs, you can identify trends and make necessary adjustments to optimize your campaigns.

Analytics tools play a pivotal role in evaluating ad performance. Platforms such as Google Analytics, Facebook Ads Manager, and other third-party tools provide comprehensive data on user interactions and ad effectiveness. These tools can help you track user engagement across various channels, including social media, email campaigns, and paid advertising. By analyzing this data, you can pinpoint which strategies are most effective in driving traffic and conversions, enabling you to refine your approach and focus on the highest-performing tactics.

ROI measurement extends beyond immediate financial returns; it encompasses the long-term value generated from customer relationships and brand loyalty. To calculate ROI accurately, consider not just the direct sales attributed to your ads but also the lifetime value of customers gained through your campaigns. This holistic view allows you to assess the broader impact of your advertising efforts, ensuring that you are not only maximizing short-term gains but also fostering a sustainable flow of consistent traffic.

Finally, the insights gained from measuring ad performance and ROI should inform future marketing strategies. By recognizing what works and what doesn't, you can allocate your budget more effectively, invest in high-impact channels, and experiment with new approaches to reach your audience. Continual improvement through measurement ensures that your business remains agile and responsive to changing market dynamics, ultimately leading to a more unstoppable flow of traffic and sustained business growth.

Chapter 7: Influencer Partnerships for Enhanced Visibility

Identifying the Right Influencers

Identifying the right influencers is crucial for businesses aiming to unlock a consistent flow of traffic. Influencers serve as bridges between brands and their target audiences, making it essential to choose individuals who align with your business values and appeal to your desired customers. To initiate this process, businesses should first define their target audience in terms of demographics, interests, and online behaviors. Understanding these characteristics allows for more precise identification of influencers who can effectively engage with your potential customers, ensuring that marketing efforts yield the highest return on investment.

Once the target audience is clearly defined, businesses can begin researching potential influencers within their niche. This involves analyzing social media platforms, blogs, and other online channels where your audience is most active. Look for influencers who have established a strong presence and possess a genuine connection with their followers. Metrics such as engagement rates, follower counts, and the overall quality of content can provide valuable insights into an influencer's effectiveness. Additionally, tools and platforms that specialize in influencer marketing can streamline this process, offering databases that categorize influencers by niche, audience demographics, and engagement metrics.

Another critical aspect of selecting the right influencer is assessing their authenticity and reputation. Influencers who prioritize transparency and foster genuine interactions tend to resonate better with their followers. It is essential to evaluate the influencer's previous partnerships and their impact on audience engagement. Businesses should seek out influencers who have a track record of successful collaborations, as this can indicate their ability to create compelling content that drives traffic. Moreover, ensuring that the influencer's values align with those of your brand will help maintain credibility and trust among your audience.

Building relationships with selected influencers is the next step in this process. Engaging with them through social media, commenting on their posts, or sharing their content can create a foundation for collaboration. It is also beneficial to approach influencers with personalized pitches that outline mutual benefits, emphasizing how the partnership can enhance their content while also driving traffic to your business. By fostering these connections, businesses can cultivate long-term partnerships that not only attract traffic but also enhance brand visibility and credibility.

Lastly, measuring the effectiveness of influencer partnerships is vital for ongoing success. After launching a campaign, businesses should utilize analytics to track traffic sources, engagement rates, and conversion metrics. This data will inform adjustments to future influencer selections and strategies, ensuring that the approach remains aligned with the business's goals. By continuously refining the influencer marketing strategy based on performance insights, businesses can maintain an unstoppable flow of traffic, ultimately leading to sustained growth and success.

Building Relationships with Influencers

Building relationships with influencers is a critical strategy for businesses aiming to unlock a consistent flow of traffic. Influencers possess established credibility and a loyal follower base, making them valuable allies in amplifying your brand's visibility. By collaborating with influencers whose audiences align with your target market, you can tap into their reach and gain access to potential customers who are already engaged and interested in similar content. This relationship goes beyond a mere transaction; it involves creating mutually beneficial partnerships that can enhance both parties' visibility and engagement.

To build effective relationships with influencers, start by identifying those who resonate with your brand values and target audience. Conduct thorough research to understand their content style, engagement metrics, and the demographics of their followers. Once you identify suitable influencers, engage with their content genuinely. This includes liking, sharing, and commenting on their posts, as well as participating in conversations related to their niche. Establishing a rapport before reaching out can make your proposal more appealing, as influencers appreciate authentic interest in their work.

Once you've built a foundation of familiarity, approach influencers with a clear and compelling value proposition. Explain how a partnership can benefit them, emphasizing the advantages such as exposure to your audience, potential for collaboration on engaging content, or even financial compensation. Be specific about what you envision for the partnership, whether it's guest blogging, social media takeovers, or co-hosting events. Providing clear, actionable ideas demonstrates that you are serious about the collaboration and have put thought into how it can be successful.

Transparency and communication are essential in nurturing influencer relationships. Clearly outline expectations from both sides, including deliverables, timelines, and compensation. Regularly check in with influencers throughout the partnership to ensure alignment and address any concerns. This ongoing dialogue fosters trust and collaboration, essential components of a long-lasting relationship. Additionally, be open to their insights and suggestions; influencers often have a deep understanding of their audience and can provide valuable feedback that can enhance your marketing efforts.

Finally, measure the impact of your influencer partnerships to refine your strategies and build upon successful collaborations. Use analytics tools to track referral traffic, engagement rates, and conversion metrics resulting from influencer campaigns. This data will not only help you assess the effectiveness of your current partnerships but also inform future collaborations. By continuously optimizing your approach based on measurable outcomes, you can create a sustainable model for leveraging influencer relationships to drive consistent and high-quality traffic to your business.

Measuring the Impact of Influencer Marketing

Measuring the impact of influencer marketing is essential for businesses aiming to attract consistent and high-quality visitors. To understand the effectiveness of influencer partnerships, businesses must establish clear metrics and key performance indicators (KPIs) that align with their marketing objectives. These metrics can include engagement rates, website traffic generated from influencer campaigns, and conversion rates attributed to influencer promotions.

By tracking these KPIs, businesses can gain insights into how influencer collaborations contribute to their overall traffic strategies and identify which influencers resonate most with their target audiences.

Another important aspect of measuring influencer marketing impact is evaluating the return on investment (ROI). This involves calculating the revenue generated as a direct result of influencer partnerships compared to the costs associated with those collaborations. Businesses should consider both direct sales and long-term value, such as brand awareness and customer loyalty, when assessing ROI. By understanding the financial implications of influencer marketing, businesses can make informed decisions about allocating resources to these partnerships and optimizing their overall marketing strategies.

In addition to quantitative metrics, qualitative assessments play a crucial role in measuring influencer marketing impact. Gathering feedback from customers who engaged with influencer content can provide valuable insights into brand perception and audience sentiment. Surveys and social media listening tools can help businesses gauge how influencer campaigns affect their brand image and customer relationships. This qualitative data complements the quantitative metrics, offering a holistic view of influencer marketing effectiveness and its contribution to driving consistent traffic.

Utilizing analytics tools is vital for measuring the impact of influencer marketing. These tools can track user behavior and engagement on websites, allowing businesses to see how visitors interact with their content after being exposed to influencer promotions. By analyzing data such as referral traffic, bounce rates, and time spent on site, businesses can identify which influencer campaigns are most successful in driving high-quality visitors. This analytical approach enables businesses to refine their influencer marketing strategies and focus on partnerships that yield the best results.

Finally, ongoing optimization is essential for maximizing the impact of influencer marketing. As businesses gather data and insights from their campaigns, they should continuously refine their approaches based on what works best. This may involve testing different types of content, varying the influencers they collaborate with, or adjusting their outreach strategies. By remaining adaptable and responsive to the data collected, businesses can unlock an unstoppable flow of traffic through influencer marketing, ensuring that their strategies remain effective in a dynamic digital landscape.

Chapter 8: Building a Strong Online Community to Boost Traffic

Engaging with Your Audience

Engaging with your audience is crucial for unlocking an unstoppable flow of traffic into your business. It is not enough to simply attract visitors; you must also ensure that they connect with your brand on a deeper level. This connection can lead to increased loyalty, repeat visits, and ultimately, higher conversion rates. To achieve this, businesses need to adopt a multifaceted approach that combines content marketing techniques, social media engagement, and personalized communication strategies.

Content marketing is one of the most effective ways to engage your audience. By creating valuable and relevant content, you can draw in potential visitors and keep them interested in your offerings. This content can take various forms, including blog posts, videos, infographics, and podcasts. It is essential to understand your target audience's preferences and pain points to produce content that resonates with them. Regularly updating your content not only helps maintain interest but also boosts your SEO efforts, increasing your visibility in search engine results and driving more traffic to your site.

Social media platforms are powerful tools for audience engagement. By actively participating in conversations, sharing relevant content, and responding to comments, businesses can foster a sense of community around their brand. Utilizing platforms like Facebook, Instagram, Twitter, and LinkedIn can significantly enhance your outreach. Tailoring your engagement strategies to fit the unique characteristics of each platform ensures that your messages are effective. Incorporating user-generated content and engaging contests can also encourage more interaction and help expand your audience reach organically.

Email marketing remains one of the most effective channels for direct communication with your audience. Crafting personalized email campaigns allows businesses to nurture leads and convert them into loyal customers. Segmenting your email list based on user behavior, preferences, and demographics enables you to send targeted messages that resonate with specific groups. Including compelling calls-to-action and exclusive offers can significantly increase engagement rates and drive traffic back to your website. Regularly analyzing the performance of your email campaigns allows for continual optimization and improvement.

Leveraging analytics is vital for understanding how to engage with your audience effectively. Tools such as Google Analytics provide insights into visitor behavior, traffic sources, and content performance. By monitoring these metrics, businesses can identify what resonates with their audience and adjust their strategies accordingly. This data-driven approach allows for informed decision-making, ensuring that your efforts to engage with your audience yield the best possible results. Implementing changes based on analytics not only enhances user experience but also optimizes traffic sources, leading to sustained growth.

Creating Valuable Community Content

Creating valuable community content is a cornerstone of attracting consistent and high-quality visitors to your business. In today's digital landscape, audiences are not just passive consumers; they actively seek out authentic connections and meaningful interactions. By focusing on community-driven content, businesses can foster engagement and loyalty, turning casual visitors into dedicated advocates. The key lies in understanding the needs and interests of your community, which can guide the creation of content that resonates with them on a personal level.

To begin crafting valuable community content, it's essential to identify the specific demographics and psychographics of your target audience. Conduct surveys, engage in social listening, and analyze existing data to uncover what your community values most. This insight allows you to tailor your content strategy, ensuring that your topics, formats, and delivery methods align with your audience's preferences. Whether it's educational articles, interactive polls, or user-generated content, the more relevant your content is, the more likely it will attract and retain visitors.

Once you have a clear understanding of your audience, consider leveraging various content formats to enhance engagement. Blog posts, videos, podcasts, and infographics each serve unique purposes and cater to different learning styles. For instance, video content can capture attention quickly and convey complex ideas succinctly, while blog posts can provide in-depth analysis and drive organic traffic through SEO optimization. By diversifying your content offerings, you can appeal to a broader audience and encourage shares across multiple platforms, ultimately expanding your reach.

Incorporating community feedback into your content creation process can significantly enhance its value. Encouraging comments, questions, and suggestions allows your audience to feel heard and valued, which deepens their connection to your brand. You can also highlight community members through features like guest posts or spotlight interviews, showcasing their expertise and experiences. This not only enriches your content but also fosters a sense of belonging within your audience, making them more likely to share your content and invite others into the conversation.

Lastly, promote your community content strategically to maximize its impact. Utilize social media channels to share snippets or highlights, engage with followers, and drive traffic back to your website. Email newsletters can be an effective way to keep your community informed about new content and encourage them to participate in discussions. Additionally, consider collaborating with influencers who align with your brand values to amplify your message and reach new audiences. By consistently delivering valuable community content and actively engaging with your audience, you can create an unstoppable flow of traffic that drives growth for your business.

Encouraging User-Generated Content

Encouraging user-generated content (UGC) is a powerful strategy for businesses looking to attract consistent and high-quality traffic. UGC not only fosters a sense of community around a brand but also serves as authentic marketing that resonates with potential customers. When users share their experiences with a product or service, they create valuable content that can enhance brand credibility. This content can take many forms, including reviews, testimonials, social media posts, and even blog entries. By actively encouraging and showcasing UGC, businesses can create a steady influx of fresh content that keeps their audience engaged and attracts new visitors.

To effectively encourage user-generated content, businesses should create platforms and opportunities for customers to share their experiences. This can be achieved through social media campaigns, contests, or dedicated sections on the company website where users can submit reviews and photos. Making it easy for customers to share their thoughts encourages participation. For instance, a simple hashtag campaign on platforms like Instagram or Twitter can motivate users to post their content while also increasing brand visibility. Businesses should also consider offering incentives, such as discounts or recognition, to motivate customers to contribute their content.

Engagement is key when it comes to user-generated content. Businesses should not only encourage users to create content but also actively engage with it. This involves responding to comments, sharing user-generated posts on official channels, and highlighting exceptional contributions. By recognizing and celebrating user contributions, businesses can foster a sense of belonging and loyalty among their audience. This engagement can lead to a cycle of continued content creation as users feel valued and motivated to share more, further driving traffic back to the business.

Incorporating UGC into marketing strategies can enhance search engine optimization (SEO) efforts as well. User-generated content often contains authentic keywords and phrases that potential customers are searching for. Additionally, fresh content is favored by search engines, which can lead to improved rankings and visibility online. By strategically integrating UGC into blog posts, product descriptions, and social media content, businesses can leverage this organic content to attract more visitors. This approach not only boosts traffic but also enhances the overall user experience by providing relatable and trustworthy information.

Lastly, building a strong online community around user-generated content can significantly impact traffic growth. Businesses should focus on creating spaces where customers feel comfortable sharing their thoughts and experiences. This could be through forums, social media groups, or community events. By nurturing this community, businesses can encourage ongoing engagement and content creation, ultimately leading to a more robust online presence. A vibrant community not only attracts new visitors but also keeps existing customers coming back, ensuring a sustainable flow of traffic that supports long-term business success.

Chapter 9: Leveraging Video Marketing for Audience Growth

Types of Video Content to Create

Video content has emerged as a powerful tool for businesses seeking to attract consistent and high-quality visitors. The diversity of video formats allows brands to engage their audience in unique ways, fostering connections that can lead to increased traffic and conversions. From educational videos to entertaining content, understanding the various types of video content can help businesses effectively convey their messages while appealing to different segments of their audience.

Tutorials and how-to videos are among the most widely sought-after types of content online. These videos provide valuable information and practical advice, positioning the creator as an authority in their niche. For businesses, creating tutorial videos can not only demonstrate products or services but also address common questions or challenges faced by potential customers. This not only helps establish credibility but also encourages viewers to visit the website for more resources, thereby driving traffic.

Another effective video type is the testimonial or case study video, which showcases satisfied customers sharing their positive experiences. These videos serve as powerful social proof, influencing potential customers' purchasing decisions. By highlighting real-life success stories, businesses can create a sense of trust and relatability that enhances their online reputation. Integrating these videos into marketing strategies can significantly boost conversion rates, as they encourage viewers to explore the brand further.

Live streaming has gained popularity as a way to foster real-time engagement with audiences. Whether it's a Q&A session, product launch, or behind-the-scenes look at the company, live videos create a sense of urgency and excitement. This interactive format allows businesses to connect with their audience directly, answering questions and addressing concerns as they arise. By promoting these live events across social media channels, businesses can attract traffic to their websites as viewers seek to engage with the content.

Finally, incorporating storytelling into video content can captivate audiences and enhance brand loyalty. Narrative-driven videos that evoke emotions or present relatable situations can resonate deeply with viewers. By sharing their brand story or the journey of their products, businesses can create a memorable experience that encourages viewers to share the content and explore the brand further. This not only aids in traffic generation but also contributes to building a community of loyal customers who are invested in the brand's success.

Distributing Video Content Effectively

Distributing video content effectively is crucial for businesses seeking to attract consistent and high-quality visitors. In an age where visual media dominates online interactions, understanding how to leverage videos can significantly enhance visibility and engagement. The key to successful video distribution lies in selecting the right platforms, tailoring content to audience preferences, and optimizing for search engines. By strategically positioning video content, businesses can create a ripple effect that drives traffic across multiple channels.

Utilizing social media platforms is one of the most effective ways to distribute video content. Each platform has its unique audience and engagement style, so tailoring video content accordingly is essential. For instance, short, attention-grabbing clips perform well on platforms like TikTok and Instagram, while longer, informative videos may thrive on YouTube or Facebook. Engaging with followers through comments and shares can amplify reach, making social media an indispensable tool in a video distribution strategy. Incorporating calls to action within the videos can further encourage viewers to visit the business's website or engage with additional content.

Email marketing remains a powerful channel for distributing video content, particularly when targeting existing customers or leads. Including video links in email campaigns can significantly increase open and click-through rates. Personalized emails that highlight the value of the video content—such as tutorials, testimonials, or product showcases—can foster a deeper connection with the audience. Additionally, segmenting email lists to tailor video content to specific demographics or interests ensures that the right message reaches the right audience, further enhancing engagement.

Search engine optimization (SEO) plays a vital role in ensuring video content is discoverable. Optimizing video titles, descriptions, and tags with relevant keywords can help videos rank higher in search engine results, increasing organic traffic. Creating a dedicated video sitemap and leveraging transcripts can also enhance SEO efforts. Furthermore, embedding videos on a website not only enriches the content but also encourages longer visit durations, which can positively impact search rankings. An effective SEO strategy for video content will lead to sustained visibility over time.

Finally, forging partnerships with influencers can dramatically expand the reach of video content. Influencers possess established audiences that trust their recommendations, making them valuable allies in a distribution strategy. Collaborating on video content or having influencers share existing videos can introduce the business to new potential customers. Additionally, building a strong online community by encouraging user-generated content or hosting live video sessions can foster engagement and loyalty, further driving traffic. By effectively distributing video content across various channels, businesses can unlock an unstoppable flow of visitors and enhance their online presence.

Analyzing Video Marketing Success

Analyzing video marketing success involves examining key performance indicators (KPIs) that reveal how well your videos are driving traffic and engagement. Metrics such as view count, watch time, and audience retention rate provide valuable insights into how effectively your content resonates with viewers. These statistics help identify which videos captivate your audience and which ones fall flat, allowing you to refine your content strategy. Moreover, tracking engagement metrics like comments, shares, and likes can indicate how well your videos are fostering community interaction and encouraging viewers to spread your message.

Another crucial aspect of video marketing analysis is understanding where your traffic is coming from. Using tools like Google Analytics can help you uncover which platforms are driving the most views and conversions. For instance, if a significant portion of your traffic originates from social media, it may be beneficial to invest more resources into promoting your videos on those channels. Conversely, if your website is the primary source of traffic, optimizing your video content for search engines can enhance visibility and drive more organic traffic.

Audience demographics also play a vital role in assessing video marketing success. Analyzing the age, gender, and location of your viewers can help tailor your future video content to better meet their interests and preferences. Understanding who engages with your videos enables you to create more targeted marketing campaigns, ensuring that your content reaches the right people. This targeted approach not only increases the chances of higher engagement but also encourages repeat visits, as audiences feel a connection to content that speaks directly to them.

The impact of video marketing on lead generation and conversion rates is another critical area to analyze. By tracking how many viewers take action after watching—such as signing up for a newsletter or making a purchase—you can gauge the effectiveness of your call-to-action strategies. A/B testing different CTAs within your videos can provide insights into what prompts your audience to take the desired steps, allowing for continual optimization of your marketing funnel. This iterative process ensures that your video content not only attracts visitors but also converts them into loyal customers.

Finally, leveraging insights gained from video marketing analysis can enhance overall content marketing strategies. By identifying successful themes, styles, and formats, you can replicate what works across other content types, such as blog posts or social media updates. Integrating video into your broader content strategy fosters a cohesive brand message and encourages cross-promotion, further amplifying your reach. Ultimately, a comprehensive approach to analyzing video marketing success empowers businesses to unlock an unstoppable flow of traffic, resulting in sustained growth and heightened visibility in competitive markets.

Chapter 10: Utilizing Analytics to Optimize Traffic Sources

Understanding Traffic Analytics Tools

Understanding Traffic Analytics Tools is crucial for businesses aiming to attract consistent and high-quality visitors. These tools provide insights into user behavior, traffic sources, and engagement metrics, allowing marketers to make data-driven decisions. By analyzing where visitors come from, how they interact with content, and the paths they take through a website, businesses can refine their strategies to optimize traffic flow. The ability to track and measure visitor engagement is essential for creating effective content marketing techniques and enhancing SEO strategies for local businesses.

Traffic analytics tools come in various forms, each offering unique features tailored to different needs. Google Analytics is one of the most widely used platforms, providing comprehensive data on website traffic, user demographics, and behavior. It helps businesses understand which marketing efforts are paying off and which need adjustment, ensuring that resources are allocated effectively. Additionally, social media analytics tools, such as Facebook Insights and Twitter Analytics, enable businesses to gauge engagement levels and audience interactions across social platforms, further informing traffic strategies.

Utilizing these analytics tools allows businesses to identify trends and patterns in visitor behavior. For instance, by monitoring bounce rates and time spent on pages, marketers can determine which content resonates most with their audience. This knowledge can drive the creation of shareable content that not only attracts visitors but also encourages them to engage more deeply with the brand. Furthermore, tracking referral traffic helps businesses understand the effectiveness of influencer partnerships and paid advertising tactics, providing a clearer picture of where to focus their marketing efforts.

Email marketing campaigns can also benefit from traffic analytics. By analyzing open rates and click-through rates, businesses can identify which messages drive the most traffic to their websites. This information allows for the refinement of email content and targeting strategies, ultimately leading to higher conversion rates. Additionally, integrating analytics with video marketing efforts can reveal viewer engagement levels, helping businesses create more compelling video content that captures audience interest and drives traffic.

In conclusion, understanding and leveraging traffic analytics tools is vital for any business looking to build an unstoppable flow of visitors. By continually monitoring and analyzing data, businesses can adapt their strategies in real-time, ensuring they meet the evolving needs of their audience. This iterative approach not only enhances traffic levels but also fosters a strong online community and drives lasting engagement, solidifying the foundation for sustainable business growth.

Identifying High-Performing Traffic Sources

Identifying high-performing traffic sources is crucial for businesses aiming to create a steady influx of visitors. The first step in this process involves analyzing current traffic patterns and understanding where visitors are coming from. Utilizing web analytics tools allows you to track the performance of different channels, such as organic search, social media, email campaigns, and paid advertising. By examining metrics like page views, bounce rates, and conversion rates, you can pinpoint which sources are delivering the most engaged visitors and which need improvement. This data is essential for making informed decisions about where to focus your marketing efforts.

Once you have a clear picture of your current traffic sources, it's important to segment them into categories based on performance. High-performing sources often include organic search due to its long-term sustainability and credibility. Analyzing the keywords that drive traffic can reveal opportunities for further optimization. Social media platforms may also rank highly, particularly if you engage with your audience effectively. By creating specific content tailored for each social media platform, you can enhance engagement and encourage shares, which can lead to increased traffic. Understanding these segments allows for a strategic approach to resource allocation.

In addition to traditional traffic sources, exploring influencer partnerships can significantly enhance visibility and attract high-quality visitors. Collaborating with influencers who align with your brand values can open doors to new audiences. Their established trust and reach can direct their followers to your business, providing a fresh stream of traffic. It's essential to identify influencers within your niche who have a genuine connection with their audience to ensure that the traffic they bring is relevant and engaged. This strategy not only boosts visibility but also lends credibility to your brand.

Furthermore, leveraging content marketing techniques is vital for attracting consistent traffic. Creating valuable, shareable content can significantly expand your reach and encourage organic sharing. This includes blog posts, infographics, and videos that resonate with your target audience. Implementing SEO best practices in your content ensures that it ranks well in search engines, driving organic traffic over time. By focusing on creating high-quality, informative content that addresses the needs and interests of your audience, you can develop a loyal following that returns to your site regularly.

Finally, regularly reviewing and optimizing your traffic sources is key to maintaining an unstoppable flow of visitors. Utilize analytics to measure the effectiveness of each source and make adjustments as needed. This may involve tweaking your email marketing campaigns, refining your social media strategy, or reallocating your advertising budget based on performance. Continuous optimization ensures that your traffic sources not only perform well but also evolve with changing market dynamics. By staying proactive and responsive to your analytics, you can sustain high-quality visitor attraction and ultimately drive business growth.

Making Data-Driven Decisions for Improvement

Making data-driven decisions is essential for businesses aiming to create an unstoppable flow of traffic. In the digital age, data serves as the backbone of effective marketing strategies. By leveraging analytics, businesses can identify which traffic sources are performing well and which are falling short. This insight allows for the optimization of marketing efforts, ensuring resources are allocated to strategies that yield the highest returns. Whether it's through organic search, social media, or paid advertising, understanding where your visitors come from can directly inform your approach to attracting consistent and high-quality traffic.

Content marketing techniques can greatly benefit from a data-driven approach. By analyzing engagement metrics such as time spent on page, bounce rates, and social shares, businesses can understand what type of content resonates with their audience. This information helps refine content strategies, enabling the creation of more targeted and effective materials. Incorporating user feedback and analytics can lead to the production of shareable content that not only attracts visitors but also encourages them to engage and convert, ultimately enhancing traffic flow.

For local businesses, SEO strategies must be tailored based on data insights. Utilizing tools that analyze local search patterns can reveal valuable keywords and phrases that potential customers are using. By optimizing website content for these specific terms, businesses can improve their visibility in local search results. Additionally, tracking the performance of these keywords over time enables ongoing adjustments to be made, ensuring that the business remains competitive in attracting local traffic.

Social media engagement also benefits significantly from data-driven decision-making. By analyzing engagement metrics across various platforms, businesses can identify which channels are most effective in driving traffic. This analysis should include monitoring the performance of different types of posts, such as images, videos, or links, to determine what garners the most interaction. Understanding audience demographics and preferences enables businesses to tailor their social media strategies, ultimately enhancing their online visibility and traffic.

Finally, employing data analytics in email marketing campaigns can lead to higher conversion rates. Analyzing open rates, click-through rates, and subscriber behavior allows businesses to segment their audience for more personalized messaging. By understanding what types of content and offers resonate with different segments, businesses can craft compelling campaigns that drive visitors to their websites. This targeted approach not only increases traffic but also fosters a loyal customer base, supporting long-term business growth.

Chapter 11: Creating Shareable Content to Expand Reach

The Elements of Shareable Content

Creating shareable content is essential for driving consistent and high-quality traffic to your business. Shareable content possesses specific characteristics that resonate with audiences, prompting them to engage and share with their networks. Understanding these elements can significantly enhance your content marketing strategy and expand your reach across various platforms. The first element is relevance. Content must be pertinent to your target audience's interests, challenges, and desires. By addressing topics that matter to your audience, you increase the likelihood of engagement and sharing.

Another crucial element of shareable content is emotional appeal. Content that evokes strong emotions—whether joy, surprise, anger, or inspiration—tends to be shared more frequently. This is because people naturally want to share experiences that resonate with them emotionally, which can also enhance their social identity. Crafting narratives or using visuals that elicit these emotions can make your content more relatable and memorable, encouraging users to pass it along to their friends and followers.

Incorporating visuals into your content is also a key element that enhances shareability. Posts with images, videos, or infographics are more engaging than text-only content. Visuals not only attract attention but also make complex information easier to digest. When users see striking visuals that complement your message, they are more likely to engage with and share the content. Thus, investing in high-quality visuals can amplify your content's reach significantly.

Another important aspect of shareable content is its originality. Unique and fresh perspectives stand out in a crowded digital landscape. When your content offers something different, whether it's a novel idea, a creative approach, or a unique take on a common topic, it captures attention and sparks curiosity. Original content encourages users to share it with their networks, as they feel they are sharing something valuable that others may not have encountered before.

Lastly, including a clear call-to-action can significantly enhance the shareability of your content. Encouraging readers to share, comment, or engage in some way can create a sense of community and participation. Whether it's asking for opinions, inviting users to share their experiences, or suggesting they pass the content along to others, a strong call-to-action can drive engagement and expand your audience. By integrating these elements into your content strategy, you can unlock an unstoppable flow of traffic to your business, making your online presence more impactful and far-reaching.

Promoting Content for Maximum Shares

Promoting content for maximum shares requires a strategic approach that aligns with the interests of your target audience while also incorporating elements that encourage engagement. To achieve this, it is essential to understand the principles of creating shareable content. Content that resonates emotionally, provides value, or offers unique insights is more likely to be shared across various platforms. A well-crafted headline and a compelling introduction can capture attention and entice readers to share the content with their networks. Utilizing storytelling techniques can make your content more relatable and memorable, increasing its chances of going viral.

In addition to creating high-quality content, optimizing it for social media platforms is crucial. Each social media channel has its own unique audience and best practices for content sharing. Tailoring your posts to fit the format and style of each platform can significantly enhance visibility. For instance, images and videos often perform better on platforms like Instagram and Facebook, while concise, engaging text might be more effective on Twitter. Utilizing hashtags strategically can also expand your reach, making it easier for users to discover your content. When content is optimized for sharing, it becomes more likely to generate organic traffic back to your website.

Engaging with your audience is another vital aspect of promoting content for maximum shares. Encourage interaction by asking questions, inviting comments, and responding promptly to feedback. Building a rapport with your audience fosters a sense of community, making them more inclined to share your content within their circles. Additionally, consider running contests or giveaways that require participants to share your content to enter. This not only boosts engagement but also amplifies your reach exponentially as participants share your content with their networks, driving more traffic to your site.

Influencer partnerships can also play a pivotal role in promoting content. Collaborating with influencers in your niche can provide access to their audience, significantly increasing the potential for shares. When selecting influencers, ensure they align with your brand values and have an engaged following. By co-creating content or having influencers share your work, you can tap into new audiences and enhance your credibility. This strategy not only increases visibility but can also lead to higher-quality traffic, as influencers often attract followers who are genuinely interested in your niche.

Finally, analyzing your content performance is essential for understanding what resonates with your audience. Utilizing analytics tools can help you track shares, engagement rates, and traffic sources, allowing you to refine your content strategy continually. By identifying which types of content generate the most shares, you can create more of what your audience loves, ultimately leading to an unstoppable flow of traffic. Regularly reviewing and adjusting your approach based on data insights ensures that your promotional efforts remain effective, maximizing your potential for consistent and high-quality visitor attraction.

Analyzing Shareability Metrics

Analyzing shareability metrics is a crucial aspect of understanding how content spreads across the digital landscape and influences traffic to your business. Shareability metrics encompass various data points that indicate how often content is shared, liked, and commented on across different platforms. These metrics provide valuable insights into audience engagement and can help businesses refine their content marketing strategies. By focusing on the right shareability metrics, businesses can identify what resonates with their audience and leverage that information to attract high-quality visitors consistently.

Key shareability metrics include social shares, engagement rates, and click-through rates. Social shares reflect how many times content has been shared on platforms like Facebook, Twitter, and LinkedIn. A high number of shares indicates that the content is not only appealing but also encourages users to share it within their networks. Engagement rates, which measure likes, comments, and shares relative to total views, provide a deeper understanding of how well content connects with its audience. Click-through rates reveal how effectively content drives traffic to a website, indicating the strength of the call-to-action and the relevance of the content to the audience's interests.

To effectively analyze these metrics, businesses should utilize various tools and analytics platforms. Social media management tools like Hootsuite or Buffer can track shares and engagement across multiple channels, while Google Analytics can provide insights into how shared content performs in terms of traffic generation. By examining these metrics over time, businesses can identify trends and patterns that highlight the types of content that yield the best results. This data-driven approach allows for continuous optimization of content strategies, ensuring that efforts are directed towards producing shareable content that attracts consistent visitors.

Understanding the demographics of those who share content is equally important. Analyzing who engages with your content can reveal valuable information regarding the target audience. This includes their interests, behaviors, and preferences, which can guide the creation of future content tailored to their needs. By segmenting the audience based on shareability metrics, businesses can develop more personalized marketing strategies that enhance engagement and drive more traffic to their websites.

Ultimately, leveraging shareability metrics not only enhances content creation but also builds a community around your brand. When content is shared widely, it increases visibility and enhances the likelihood of attracting new visitors who are interested in your brand's offerings. By fostering an environment where audiences feel compelled to share and engage with content, businesses can unlock an unstoppable flow of traffic, maintaining a cycle of consistent visitor attraction that drives growth and success.

www.ingramcontent.com/pod-product-compliance
Lightning Source LLC
Chambersburg PA
CBHW070958240526
45469CB00017B/2464